7 MOMENTS
THAT WILL IGNITE YOUR
FAITH

LISA SORIANO, LCSW

7 MOMENTS THAT WILL IGNITE YOUR FAITH

LISA SORIANO, LCSW

7 Moments That Will Ignite Your Faith

© 2023 Lisa Soriano

Published by HigherLife Development Services, Inc.
PO Box 623307
Oviedo, FL 32762
(407) 563-4806
www.ahigherlife.com

ISBN: 978-1-958211-47-2 hardback
ISBN: 978-1-958211-46-5 paperback
ISBN: 978-1-958211-48-9 ebook
Library of Congress case no. 2023909614

Printed in the United States of America
10 9 8 7 6 5 4 3 2 1

Let the redeemed of the Lord tell their story.

—Psalm 107:2

*I want you all to know about the miraculous signs and wonders
the Most High God has performed for me. How great are His signs,
how powerful His wonders! His kingdom will last forever,
His rule through all generations.*

—Daniel 4:2–3 NLT

Dedication

This book is dedicated with love to my husband, children, family, and friends, in addition to all of you who've chosen to pick this book up. The important message I really want to get out to all of you is to remember that your life is a gift that was birthed into this world, filled with purpose, gifts, talents, and a calling, given to you by God. Although life can have its ups and downs, it's important to remember you will get through if you stay in and do not lose heart or give up. We can think of life being like a journey. We are all a work in progress. So, please keep your head up. There is hope. It's not about how you started life, as some of us had tough beginnings, but more about how you finish. Remember that we are all running this race called life, and you still have a race to complete to cross that finish line. No matter what setbacks you may face, running off track at times or continuing what seems like a long, rocky road as life throws challenges your way—remember that you are not in this race of life alone. You are here for a reason. Sometimes things or people can appear to be a heavy weight dragging them down or off course, but the good news is that whether this takes place or not, you can get through it all with God. With that, I encourage you not to give up. Keep going. It will be worth it!

> *Therefore, since we are surrounded by such a huge crowd of witnesses to the life of faith, let us strip off every weight that slows us down, especially the sin that so easily trips us up. And let us run with endurance the race God has set before us. We do this by keeping our eyes on Jesus, the champion who initiates and perfects our faith. Because of the joy awaiting Him, He endured the cross, disregarding its shame. Now He is seated in the place of honor beside God's throne.*
>
> —Hebrews 12:1–3 NLV

Acknowledgments

Special thanks to my aunt Rhonda Sciortino, who gifted me with how to write and publish a book, and to my dear friend and mentor, Marnie Nunnally, for helping me in the editorial phase of the manuscript prior to submission for publishing. To Marnie Nunnally, Ms. Sherry Gibbs, and Victoria Pontell, for constantly pouring out encouragement and being there as spiritual mentors, and all of you who came around me for support throughout the entire process. I would also like to thank my project manager, Marcy Pusey, for her spiritual guidance and encouragement. Love you all.

Contents

I PLANTED THE SEED,
APOLLOS WATERED IT, BUT
GOD HAS BEEN MAKING IT
GROW. SO, NEITHER THE
ONE WHO PLANTS NOR
THE ONE WHO WATERS
IS ANYTHING, BUT ONLY
GOD, WHO MAKES THINGS
GROW.

–1 Corinthians 3:6

Preface

Did you grow up in a household where religion was important in your family? Was religion something that was forced onto you at a young age? Maybe you grew up like I did, in a home where religion or God wasn't talked about much, if ever. There are many ways that we are raised, either being told about the existence of God or maybe never being talked to about God at all. Either way, you may have reached a point when you started questioning if God was real. You may think, *"If there is a God, which religion is true?"* Or maybe that hasn't even come to mind. You may even be agnostic or atheist. Overall, we are all on a journey of some sort, and part of our journey may include questioning God's existence. So, no matter where you are in life, I hope that there is something you can gain by reading this book.

Both my parents and stepparents raised me. Neither set of my parental figures exposed us to much religion. Praying was only done in our home for a holiday gathering, before a meal, or a special occasion. Those were usually short prayers to bless the meal we were about to eat; longer prayers didn't happen. It was usually a "hurry up and make it short so we can eat" prayer. I can't remember a time when my family talked about spiritual things. It was more about the saying, "You could do anything you want to if you put your mind to it," which may be how you grew up. Most of my biological father's side was Catholic, and most of my biological mother's side was Mormon. However, my parents divorced when I was five, so I did not attend church much unless it was a special occasion or holiday. My maternal grandmother tried her best to expose us to the Mormon religion, and I was baptized Mormon at the age of sixteen but left the church shortly after that. I was young and didn't stay interested. I don't blame my parents or think negatively about them because of this. My story may not be like yours—we all

PREFACE

grow up differently. Whether we were raised in homes hearing about God or not, I think there comes a point when we start to question if God is real. I believe that when you reach an age where you begin to think more for yourself, you might start to view the world outside of your caregiver's views. I know I did, especially after going through many challenges and heartbreaks in my earlier adult years that had me seeking answers and needing peace and direction.

I started wondering if God was real, which led me on this faith journey, which you will discover while reading this book.

CALL TO ME
AND I WILL ANSWER
YOU, AND I WILL TELL
YOU GREAT AND MIGHTY
THINGS, WHICH YOU DO
NOT KNOW.

—Jeremiah 33:3 NASB

GIVE THANKS TO THE
LORD AND PROCLAIM
HIS GREATNESS. LET THE
WHOLE WORLD KNOW
WHAT HE HAS DONE. SING
TO HIM; YES, SING HIS
PRAISES. TELL EVERYONE
ABOUT HIS WONDERFUL
DEEDS.

—1 Chronicles 16:8–9 NLT

CHAPTER 1

The Crystal Beaded Necklace

I discovered I was pregnant a few days shy of my nineteenth birthday. At the time, I was living in Colorado with my mother. I felt defeated by the thought of becoming a young mom because several of my loved ones suggested I was too young and should consider having an abortion. However, no matter how scary the thought of having a baby was, I knew I would not terminate my pregnancy by having an abortion. I would never judge anyone who has had an abortion or is considering one … this is just part of my journey.

Although young, unmarried, and not in a healthy, emotionally mature place, I intentionally tried to get pregnant. I had been in a relationship for about six months with the father of my unborn baby. He was my dream guy, and I was madly in love with him and wanted a future with him. I worshipped him; he was my everything. Our relationship was intense with romance and chemistry; however, we were both young and not really in a position to be parents. My emotional immaturity quickly got in the way of continuing the relationship, which led to our breakup shortly after the birth of our son.

The separation and breakup were devastating. My son's father and I came to a point where it didn't seem like we would stay together and raise our son as a couple. When we broke up, our son was eight months old. His father served me custody papers, wanting sole custody. It was devastating, as I never wanted to raise our son out of wedlock, and I did not want him to grow up in a separate household. I was raised in a two-family home, and it wasn't easy. I never wanted my son to experience being raised that way. It shattered my dream of having a family. I was completely broken inside and wanted so badly to remain with his father and raise our son as a family, but my dream of having a family of my own was shattered.

During that difficult time, I felt alone, with no support. My family loved me but thought it best to stay out of it and let me handle everything because I was an adult. Although it was difficult then, I do not harbor any resentment toward them. They did what they thought was best. As days passed, I began believing the lie in my head that my son would be better off without me. I was a mess. I had so much growing up and inner healing to do and, to be honest, I had no mental and emotional equipment to bring a child into my messy life and raise him. I felt horrible as a human being and as a young mom. However, I knew his father had extremely supportive parents who loved our son, and up until the point of separation, they'd helped us financially and by sharing their home. They were there to guide and support us.

When I was served the custody papers, I thought his father would do better raising him. I signed the documents granting him sole custody. It was one of my most difficult decisions and times. In my mind, I had failed as a mother. The ridicule and judgment from people I faced afterward were extremely painful. Whether it was said to me directly or not, it was felt. I had thoughts of ending my life but was too terrified to do so. Instead, I decided I needed to do whatever I could to try and become the best person I could be for our son. I also secretly hoped that my son's father and I could one day make it work and be a family.

After I signed the custody papers, I was emotionally broken down. I decided to fly back to California, where one of my biggest support persons lived: my paternal grandmother. She's now been deceased for twenty-one years. She was one of the people in my life who showed me unconditional love. No matter how badly I messed up, she was always there for me, ready to give the shirt off her back. I am so grateful for her unconditional steadfast love in my life.

My goal in moving to California was to better my life, be in a supportive environment to heal emotionally, and get educated to gain a professional career with benefits. I wanted to provide a better life for my son, and I believed I could do that by getting an education and a professional career as a Medical Assistant. However, I

In my mind, I had failed as a mother. The ridicule and judgment from people that I faced afterward were extremely painful. Whether it was said to me directly or not, it was felt.

knew I also needed a lot of emotional healing. My life was in shambles. I did not want our son to grow up in a divided household. So, with a heart heavy with sadness, I moved to California, believing it would be temporary—just long enough to complete the year's program, gain emotional maturity, and reunite in Colorado with my son and his father.

As if signing the sole custody papers was not enough, getting on the airplane that day was the second most difficult decision I have ever made. I experienced my very first separation panic attack. I'd never had a panic attack, but as soon as I stepped foot on that airplane, I felt panic and a deep sorrow overwhelm me as I separated myself from my son. I felt like such a horrible mother. How could a mother leave her child like that? I'll tell you, when you are in a state of mind like I was, so desperate and broken, you are not able to think rationally.

A week after arriving in California, I decided to drive to Barnes & Noble Bookstore, about five minutes from my grandmother's home where I was living. It was a heavy and emotional time, and I was in a bit of a funk. I needed some guidance and encouragement. I had been on a mission, seeking answers to my future and some hope and guidance to help me because the heavy feelings of guilt, shame, anxiety, and despair consumed me.

I pulled into a parking space and sat parked momentarily as I tried to motivate myself to open the door and walk inside. I mean, who wants to be around people in public when you feel like you could literally break down in tears at any given moment? I sat there discouraged and lost in my thoughts, then happened to glance over. For some reason, I focused on the crystal-beaded necklace on my review mirror, where I hung it when I wasn't wearing it. The necklace was something I wore to feel secure and a sense of happiness because it reminded me of the good times I had when I wore it. In a bizarre way, the necklace gave me hope and reminded me that good days would come.

You probably know what the rosary beads of the Catholic faith are—the ones you sometimes see hanging inside people's cars, usually wrapped around the review mirrors. I remember glancing over to the car to my left and seeing rosary beads hanging tightly around their review mirror. Immediately, the thought came through my mind (I had no idea why at the time), *Wouldn't it be cool if my necklace was wrapped around tightly like their rosary beads?*

I dismissed the passing thought and slowly entered Barnes & Noble. I planned to look up my and my son's father's horoscopes to determine if there was hope for us and find some direction. As I mentioned, my mother's side of the family was Mormon, and my father's was Catholic. My father converted to Mormonism when he married my mother, but when I was five years old, my parents divorced, and from that point on, I wasn't exposed to any religion regularly—or God, for that matter. I always knew in the back of my mind that something was out there, but again, I never experienced God personally.

I found some books on different horoscopes and how certain signs got along in intimate relationships with others. It was intriguing. After about an hour of research, I returned to my car to go home. When I got into my car and sat down, I was immediately drawn back to my beaded necklace.

My necklace was wrapped tightly around my rearview mirror. I sat there for about 10 seconds, wondering how that could be. I didn't do it, and nobody else was with me or heard me think that thought when I got out of my car.

I looked back to the car I initially saw parked to my left, which was no longer there. I tried to undo the necklace, thinking, *How did this happen?* It was so tightly tied around the rearview mirror that I thought, *Oh my gosh, this is absolutely crazy.*

Immediately after that, I had a thought enter my mind. It was not audible or anything I could hear, but it was a still small voice in my mind. I heard clearly, "Don't worry; everything will be okay." I felt immense chills all over my body, like a divine or angelic presence was in my car. It was as if I had electricity surging through my body. That was the first time I had ever experienced anything like that. That was the very first moment that I knew there had to be something out there, be it God or an angel or something, but there was something bigger than me that I couldn't see, that was real, and it moved my beaded necklace as a sign, a spoken word of hope and faith.

It planted the seed of faith in me. It led me on a path to seek more. I wanted to experience more of that. So, I began chasing after it, wanting to find what it was and know God, if there was one. I knew that there was *something* out there for that to happen. There had to be a God.

I attended a local Catholic church for the next six months because I had heard their church masses were short, and I was on a mission to learn more about God. I wanted to hear more of the voice I'd heard that day in my car, giving me so much inner peace. The voice that told me not to worry and that everything was going to be okay.

Attending weekly masses at the Catholic church fizzled out as I lost interest and didn't find what I was seeking. I put my seeking on hold and stopped attending church. Being a part of the Catholic faith doesn't mean you're on the wrong path or don't believe in God. We're all on a journey in life, and each person may find their path leads in a different direction. I know many born-again Christians who've decided to stay in the Catholic faith because it is their home of worship and where they feel comfortable. That's between them and God. I'm talking more about entering into a relationship with our Creator when I say becoming a "born-again Christian" and praying the sinner's prayer. This isn't to put down any faith or religion.

Looking back now, I can see the supernatural and mysterious ways God worked to use my necklace, being tied tightly around my review mirror, moving the necklace, and then giving me that comforting word that everything would be okay. That was where the first seed was planted, giving me faith that God existed—I just didn't know Him yet.

SOMETHING TO CONSIDER

Have you ever wondered if God is real? Are you seeking to know more about God? I want to challenge you to seek Him. Whether you grew up in a household where religion was discussed or not, there may come to a point in your life, like now, where something is stirring inside, and you think, *"Could this actually be real?"*

You may also think, *"This is crazy; she had to have moved that necklace."* I get it. I was shocked to experience it! But I would like to challenge you to take it all in and pray—ask God to reveal Himself in a special way to you. It may not be how He revealed Himself to me, but I know God does not favor anyone and loves everyone. If you genuinely want to experience God in a real and tangible way, He will show up for you in a way you will receive. It may be when you least expect it, but if you genuinely want to know if God is real and have a personal encounter, I urge you to get going on your seeking.

SEEK THE LORD YOUR
GOD, [AND] YOU WILL
FIND HIM IF YOU SEEK HIM
WITH ALL YOUR HEART
AND WITH ALL YOUR SOUL.

—Deuteronomy 4:29

AND YOU WILL SEEK ME
AND FIND ME, WHEN YOU
SEARCH FOR ME WITH ALL
YOUR HEART.

—Jeremiah 29:13 NASB

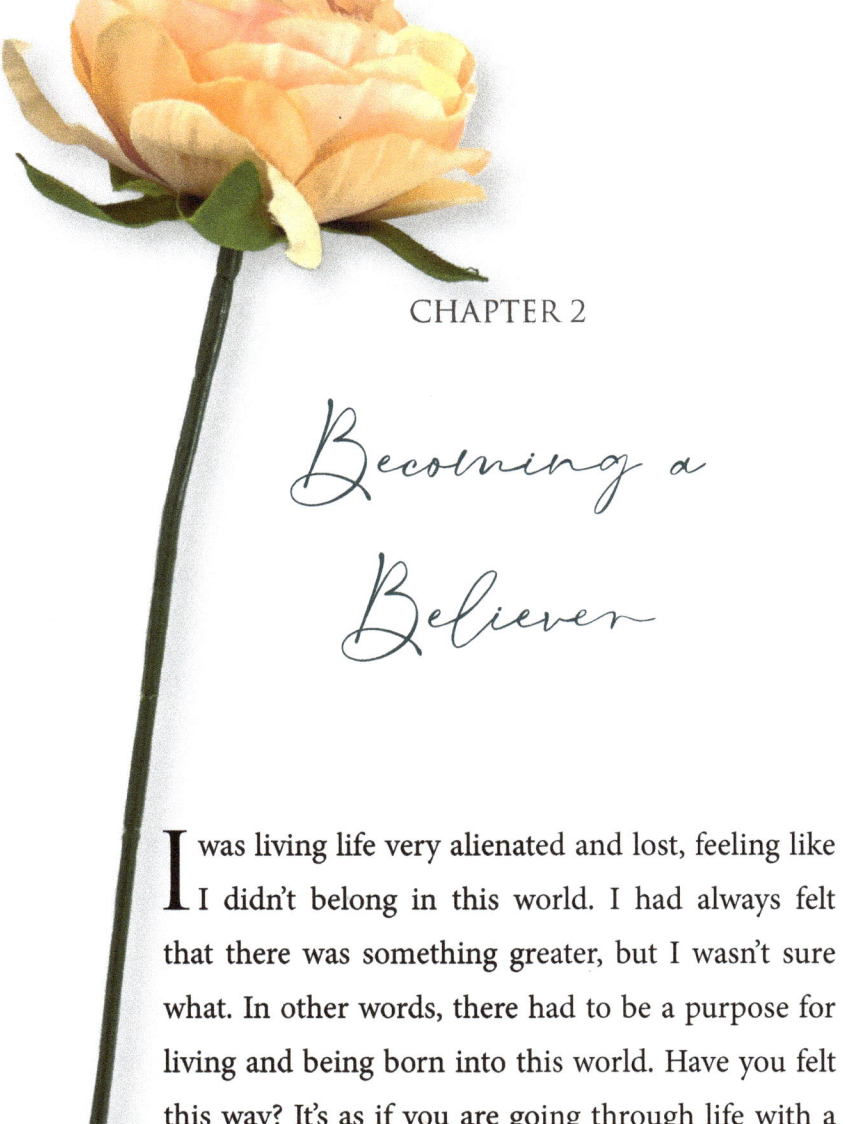

CHAPTER 2

Becoming a Believer

I was living life very alienated and lost, feeling like I didn't belong in this world. I had always felt that there was something greater, but I wasn't sure what. In other words, there had to be a purpose for living and being born into this world. Have you felt this way? It's as if you are going through life with a feeling of not entirely belonging and feeling that there must be more to life than getting up, going to school or work, or staying at home and ending your day, only to repeat it over and over every day. You may have everything that money can buy, feel full of freedom when purchasing whatever your heart desires, or feel happy, have your health, and yet still feel a void within you. No matter how much you have, it may never seem enough. It may feel as though nothing good truly lasts. There is always something you still want, making it hard to remain content, which leaves you feeling empty or as though you need more satisfaction or peace.

I felt something similar in my life. I felt like no matter how hard I tried to better myself, brush myself off from heartache, loss, and emotional pain, nothing fully helped or was sustaining. Nothing could take the pain away or fill the void that I felt deep within me. It got even worse when life slowed down, and I was left to myself without any distractions. It was as if I failed at everything I tried to do, and I got easily discouraged. I could not get it together; it seemed like a slippery slope. I would get up and try to shake things off in my own strength, regain some thought process regarding a given situation, and try to move forward but struggled every time. The struggle was worst when I felt alone and as if nothing could truly satisfy me or take the emotional pain away. It seems like the most challenging time was when my son's father and I broke up, and I was faced with custody papers. I felt utterly lost, broken, hopeless, and full of guilt and shame. How could I, a mother, walk away from my child and not fight for my son?

On top of that, I felt extremely judged by many and left alone. That constant guilt left me with a strong feeling of being a failure and hopeless. Although I believed I had made the best decision for my son at that time, I still beat myself up over it constantly. I just kept thinking it was temporary, and I wanted to better my life for my son and possibly his father, hoping to reunite with them and have our little family. So, I focused on getting an education that would land me in a career where I could provide a better life for him, having a job and more financial stability. I lived with my paternal grandmother, and she supported me financially so that I could make this goal happen. After nine months, I received my certificate as a Medical Assistant and worked on and off for several medical practices, but I wasn't stable in that for long. I returned to waiting tables because I had shorter shifts and made decent money. However, I constantly struggled emotionally and eventually became a hot mess. I was so broken down inside; however, I continued to act strong and as if I was okay, but I was definitely not. I was good at faking it, or what some would call "persevering."

I got down on myself, mentally tearing myself down, which was usually before bedtime when things would quiet down—when I was alone and not distracted by something. The love of my life was not interested in me at all. I had walked away from mothering my child. My grandmother, who was my everything, had now passed away. I had a mental breakdown and could not find peace or stability. I was all over the place physically and mentally.

When times were tough, I was reminded of that beaded necklace situation in my car five years prior. It came back to my memory from time to time. At this point in my life, I had been couch-hopping. I was living at my sister's for a few days, occupying her guest bedroom, and then back to one of two of my friend's houses for a few days. I was waiting tables at a local restaurant, trying to earn enough money to pay the bills but not really saving anything. I don't think I was even paying any bills, if I am truly honest. I was not on drugs and did not drink, but

No matter how much you have, it may never seem enough. It may feel as though nothing good truly lasts. There is always something you still want, making it hard to remain content, which leaves you feeling empty or as though you need more satisfaction or peace.

I did smoke cigarettes. I quit while pregnant to ensure I didn't pass anything toxic on to my unborn child, but I quickly picked the habit back up after giving birth. I had been a smoker since the age of sixteen.

In June 2000, I lost my way and had a mental breakdown, six months after I'd decided it might be better to leave my child's life completely. It was triggered by depriving my body of fat for five years, being anorexic, and weighing only eighty-eight pounds. I was only five feet five wearing a size double zero in clothing, and the clothes were still baggy. I was on a mission to win back my son's father and thought that if I got skinnier and made something of my life, got smarter and maintained a career, maybe he would want me and want our family back together again. I was working two jobs. I worked as a make-up artist for Clinique on the weekends and as a Medical Assistant full-time during the week. I was going out dancing four nights a week and finally just had a mental breakdown. It was a pivotal moment in my life. It led me on a further journey of self-discovery and seeking peace for months or years, but I could never figure out how to obtain it.

I had lost my way and ended up having a mental breakdown.

At the beginning of May 2002, I woke up at 4:00 a.m. and was inspired to write in my journal. Please keep in mind, I wasn't one to wake up during the middle of the night, nor one to journal during this time of my life. I was a heavy sleeper. I had no idea what the Holy Spirit was, but for some reason, I had woken up and was inspired to write down who the Holy Spirit was in my journal. I wrote and wrote and wrote for pages, and then after about an hour of writing super-fast, I went right back to sleep. I remember writing in detail about who the Holy Spirit, God, and Jesus were.

A month later, I was at the gym like I usually would be and happened to run into an old acquaintance. It was a guy I had dated briefly when I was sixteen, back in 1992. Here we were, ten years later, reuniting at the gym. I was emotionally lost, broken inside, feeling like I was damaged goods, and desperately needing peace. However, no matter how bad I felt, I still believed that I was an attractive young woman and that men were attracted to me wherever I went. So, there I was, breaking a sweat on the stair climber, and he came up and started talking to me. We were both shocked and happy to have run into one another. I was a bit embarrassed. I was drenched with sweat and out of breath because I was in the middle of a workout, and who knows how I smelled. We greeted each other and tried to catch up quickly on what we had been doing over the past ten years as I continued on my stair climber machine. He was always an attractive and friendly guy. I was even thinking about how attractive he still was. Anyway, after we said our hello's, he asked me out for coffee to catch up more outside the gym and without distraction. I remember thinking, *Here's another guy interested in me,* as I was pretty full of myself and confident for the most part. Although I had many insecurities, I felt I was a pretty girl with a nice body. I lacked confidence regarding who I was inside, knowing I was an emotional mess needing much healing. At this point in my life, I was fueled by getting attention from men. In other words, my self-worth and validation came from how much attention I got. I was already talking to four different guys then, and now he would be the fifth.

We met at a local coffeehouse a few days later to catch up. I remember sitting there, a bit nervous, thinking, *What will we talk about?* I took out my cigarette, asking him if he would mind if I had a smoke. He said he didn't mind at all. So, I began smoking as he talked to me about

I remember writing in detail about who the Holy Spirit, God, and Jesus were.

how his life had been transformed, how good God was, and how much peace he had. His facial expression and overall confidence showed me that he was full of joy and peace. A joy and peace that I was so thirsty for and had never experienced in my life. More specifically, as soon as he mentioned the word peace, it was as if everything in my body stood at attention and wanted more. I wanted what he had. It was as if I was pierced in my heart and mind and woken up from the dead. An excitement rose in me that I had never felt. I wanted and needed peace for so long and never knew how to get it, and it seemed like he had the secret. He had the treasure that I had been longing and searching for. I would only feel peaceful occasionally, but it was fleeting. I wanted that so badly for myself. I was desperate to hear more, like a parched animal finally finding a stream of water.

I immediately asked him how I could get the peace he spoke of. By the look on his face, he seemed thrilled that I asked. He was happy to share how I could get the peace he described. He told me how he got peace from having a personal relationship with Jesus Christ. He explained that I could get that peace by asking Jesus to come into my life and how amazing it would be. He said that Jesus

I was fueled by getting attention from men.

could instill His perfect peace in me—that Jesus was the Prince of Peace and wanted to give me peace and that all I needed to do was ask. He said we can sometimes experience peace in life, but the peace he described was like no other. He said his life had been full of peace and contentment because of his relationship with Jesus. He explained how I could enter into a relationship with Jesus and instructed me on how to pray. He said to go home and pray to Jesus, tell Jesus that I believe that He came to the world to die on the cross so that I could have eternal life, and then invite Jesus to be the Lord and Savior of my life, inviting Him into my heart. Honestly, I was like, *Are you flat kidding me? This is seriously sounding super crazy*, but for some reason, it felt good. It felt like I had been thirsty for years, and he offered me the coldest refreshing drink. I'd thought this coffee date was an actual date because he was interested in me; however, it turned into a date with Jesus. Jesus was the one that was inviting me into an intimate, forever relationship with Him. Not only did this friend just give me an eternal gift, but he also gave me a Bible to start reading after I prayed that prayer. He bought me a New Living Translation Life Application Bible that night. He said it was a great Bible and easy to understand.

He said that Jesus could instill His perfect peace in me—that Jesus was the Prince of Peace and wanted to give me peace and that all I needed to do was ask.

I left the coffee shop full of excitement and eagerness. I wanted to get home to a private place and pray that special prayer, inviting Jesus to come into my heart and be the Lord of my life. I also prayed for Him to remove everything from my life that was not His plan or will for my life because I did not want to live for myself anymore. I was exhausted from repeating the same mistakes, which left me feeling empty and defeated.

That day, June 13, 2002, was the day that changed the course of my life and destiny forever. It was amazing what happened next. It was as if I had been walking around blind all those years, and now, I could really see. I had a spiritual awakening. I instantly felt a sense of belonging and purpose—joy and excitement like I had never experienced. I was excited to be on this new journey and deeply yearned to learn more about God. I immediately wanted to read my new Bible. He told me to start in the New Testament Book of John.

In the past, I could never push myself to stay interested in reading the Bible. I had family members buy me Bibles over the years; however, I never felt urged to pick it up and read. It was so difficult even to want to read, and when I did try, which was usually during a tough time, it

It was as if I had been walking around blind all these years, and now, I could really see. I had a spiritual awakening.

felt like I was reading a history book, which completely bored me.

Surprisingly, after praying that prayer, I realized I did not want to stop reading the Bible. I could not and did not want to put it down. I also cannot fully describe how the immense inner peace of belonging, like being a part of something so big, was immediately instilled in me when I prayed that prayer. The peace is unlike the temporary peace we feel when things go peacefully or well. It is powerful and completely different.

There were so many radically instant transformations that took place in my life. It was quite shocking how quickly things were happening. The most instantaneous was losing the immediate desire to smoke cigarettes. I used to enjoy smoking about a pack of cigarettes a day. The next morning after I prayed that prayer, I tried to do my regular daily routine of smoking in the morning when I woke up, and I almost vomited. It made me extremely nauseous. I was completely shocked. How could I be so repulsed by something that I usually loved doing? My repulsion was so bad that I immediately threw them away. It was evident that the prayer I prayed to remove everything from my life that was not God's will for me had indeed worked. To this day, I have never smoked another cigarette. It was an instant transformation and nothing of my doing. I literally could not stand the smell of cigarettes. That was alarming evidence that God is real and powerful and can miraculously deliver people from their addictions because He did it for me.

I prayed for God to remove everything from my life, including the men I was talking to, because I only desired His will to take over my life. I wanted to live a surrendered life, knowing that I did not make the best decisions and needed His divine intervention and guidance, especially in selecting the men I would be intimately involved with. Believe it or not, these guys who'd been calling me daily suddenly stopped calling. I even thought, *How is that possible?* I started questioning, *What did I do?* but then quickly remembered that I prayed for God to take the desire of these people away and for them to stop calling me if He didn't want them in my life. Sure enough, they stopped calling, and I never spoke to them again. That was another profound way that God moved on my behalf, to show me His divine intervention. That prayer of asking Jesus to come into my life and transform me and for me to follow Him and His will for my life was transformative.

BECOMING A BELIEVER

It is vital to share that as I continued my journey and cultivated my relationship with God more, I discovered the true meaning of being a Christian. It's not about attending church in a building like some of us may have heard growing up, but all about entering into a real relationship with our Creator. We are designed to have citizenship in Heaven, and once we enter into God's Kingdom by receiving and believing in Him, we become an ambassador in His Kingdom. We are part of a royal family here on Earth and are passing through until we make it into our eternal heavenly homes. So, feeling like an outsider was probably accurate for how I felt until I got the invitation to become a part of something bigger than me, a Kingdom, an eternal Kingdom, and that's why I no longer felt lost and like an outsider.

The beauty of God's love is that He gives us free will to choose whether or not we want to believe in Him. He is not a forceful God but invites us all into a relationship with Him. I found that the void and feelings of being an outsider and not quite finding my belonging or purpose was all placed in me from the beginning. God intentionally created us with a void for Him to fill, but again, we have a choice to invite Him in and believe in Him.

SOMETHING TO CONSIDER

You may be asking what it means to enter into a relationship with Jesus and be a born-again Christian. Here is the Scripture reference on how to become a born-again believer. You may feel that you have not belonged to anything or exist with no real purpose. If you are tired of living life feeling like you want more and want to belong to the Kingdom of God, please pray first and read the Scripture verses below. There is a prayer at the back of this book that you can then pray to invite Jesus into your life and heart and become a born-again, spiritually born human. The Holy Spirit will then be sent to you as a guide to lead and instruct you on all truth. You will feel like a veil was removed from your mind and eyes and like a new person with a completely different perspective—a heavenly perspective that will be sealed into your heart and mind. Please continue to read on to see what exactly the Bible has to say about what I am sharing:

Now there was a Pharisee, a man named Nicodemus who was a member of the Jewish ruling council. He came to Jesus at night and said, "Rabbi, we know that You are a teacher who has come from God. For no one could perform the signs You are doing if God were not with him."

Jesus replied, "Very truly I tell you, no one can see the kingdom of God unless they are born again."

"How can someone be born when they are old?" Nicodemus asked. "Surely they cannot enter a second time into their mother's womb to be born!"

Jesus answered, "Very truly I tell you, no one can enter the kingdom of God unless they are born of water and the Spirit. Flesh gives birth to flesh, but the Spirit gives birth to spirit. You should not be surprised at my saying, 'You must be born again.' The wind blows wherever it pleases. You hear its sound, but you cannot tell where it comes from or where it is going. So it is with everyone born of the Spirit."

"How can this be?" Nicodemus asked.

"You are Israel's teacher," said Jesus, "and do you not understand these things? Very truly I tell you, we speak of what we know, and we testify to what we have seen, but still you people do not accept

our testimony. I have spoken to you of earthly things and you do not believe; how then will you believe if I speak of heavenly things? No one has ever gone into heaven except the one who came from heaven—the Son of Man. Just as Moses lifted up the snake in the wilderness, so the Son of Man must be lifted up, that everyone who believes may have eternal life in him" (John 3:1–14).

For this is how God loved the world: He gave His one and only Son, so that everyone who believes in Him will not perish but have eternal life. God sent His Son into the world not to judge the world, but to save the world through Him.

—John 3:16–17 NLT

HE HAS MADE
EVERYTHING BEAUTIFUL IN
ITS TIME. HE HAS ALSO SET
ETERNITY IN THE HUMAN
HEART; YET NO ONE CAN
FATHOM WHAT GOD HAS
DONE FROM BEGINNING
TO END.

—Ecclesiastes 3:11

WE ARE THEREFORE
CHRIST'S AMBASSADORS,
AS THOUGH GOD WERE
MAKING HIS APPEAL
THROUGH US.
WE IMPLORE YOU ON
CHRIST'S BEHALF: BE
RECONCILED TO GOD.
GOD MADE HIM WHO
HAD NO SIN TO BE SIN
FOR US, SO THAT IN HIM
WE MIGHT BECOME THE
RIGHTEOUSNESS
OF GOD.

—2 Corinthians 5:20–21

I WILL GIVE YOU A NEW
HEART AND PUT A NEW
SPIRIT WITHIN YOU; I
WILL TAKE THE HEART OF
STONE OUT OF YOUR FLESH
AND GIVE YOU A HEART
OF FLESH. I WILL PUT
MY SPIRIT WITHIN YOU
AND CAUSE YOU TO WALK
IN MY STATUTES, AND YOU
WILL KEEP MY JUDGMENTS
AND DO THEM.

—Ezekiel 36:26–27 NKJV

CHAPTER 3

The Test from the Dark Side

Be alert and of sober mind. Your enemy the
devil prowls around like a roaring lion looking
for someone to devour.

—1 Peter 5:8

When my older son was five years old, I encouraged my son's father to move out to Southern California. Both of us had many relatives living there. I was happy he agreed to move and settle in the Los Angeles area. At that time, I moved back into my mother and stepfather's home, located forty miles east of Los Angeles. I was living with them to save money to afford my own apartment. I sought a job in Los Angeles as a Medical Assistant. I was thinking that if I worked near where my son lived, I would be able to be more involved in his life, seeing him more than just on the weekends. Thankfully, his father and I were always able to communicate for the most part, and he was always willing to work with me, never withholding our son from me. During this time, he was nice enough to allow me to pick my son up and take him to school, and then after work, I would hang out at their home regularly to spend time with my son while I waited for the traffic on the freeways to die down. It was a blessing, and I am thankful for that time and that his father was willing to allow me more time with our son.

One particular afternoon, after I had picked our son up from school, I decided to take my son to the grocery store near their home to grab some groceries. We went into the grocery store, laughing and having a great time together. After picking up a few things, we headed back to the parking garage to return to their home. I opened the door for my son to get in the car, and as I made my way around the car, I was approached by a young girl. She couldn't have been more than eight years old. She told me that she could tell me the future of my life. My first thought was, *Where in the world is this little girl's parent or an adult watching her, and why would they allow her to approach a stranger like me?*

So, I said, "I'm sorry, but are you with an adult?" She immediately yelled for her mother to come to my car, saying, "Mommy, Mommy, she is asking to talk to you." I looked up to see if I could see her mother. There, off in the distance, about twenty feet away, I saw a woman walking toward me. As she approached me, she dove into telling me that she could help me figure out my life and wanted to tell me my future—that she was a fortune teller.

Interestingly, I had just read about sorcery, witchcraft, and fortune tellers in the Old Testament book of Deuteronomy. I quickly remembered how those things were stated as an abomination to the Lord. I was a bit freaked out, to be honest, and not just for my safety but mostly for my son, who was safely locked inside the car, patiently waiting and probably wondering what was going on. I wanted to get out of there so quickly; my heart was racing, and I was overwhelmed with a feeling of evil. I knew deep down that this woman was not good.

I also knew that I had a responsibility to honor God and not listen to anything that she had to say, as I had just read in my Bible that had I continued to be intrigued and listened to her that it was an abomination to the Lord. So, I immediately said I was not interested in listening to anything she said. I wanted to get out of there quickly. I had the chills all over my body, but not the good chills. I had a bad feeling that I was not to entertain anything she had to say, so I quickly shut the conversation down by telling her that my son was in the car and we needed to leave. I thanked her out of fear and wanting to escape and quickly got in my car and left the parking garage without looking back. I remember my son asking me what happened and who that lady and little girl were, but I just said, "Oh, they were just trying to sell something, but I was not interested." He was content with that answer, and we quickly drove back to their home. I felt a bit eerie and out of sorts, but I also knew I needed to be present for my son and not show any signs of fear from me, not to have him worry. We both went about our evening and enjoyed

I also knew that I had a responsibility to honor God and not listen to anything that she had to say, as I had just read in my Bible that had I continued to be intrigued and listened to her that it was an abomination to the Lord.

the rest of our time together before I had to drive back home.

Fast forward to the very next day. I went to work like any typical day. I often left my parents' home by 4:00 a.m. to avoid the traffic into Los Angeles, which was always a nightmare if you didn't get on the road before 5:00 a.m. After my morning workout at the gym, I would pick up my son, take him to school, and then head to work, about five miles from his school. After three hours of working that day, I began to experience a horrible headache and was urged by the physicians I worked for to take 800 mg of ibuprofen. I took their advice on an empty stomach, which was not smart. The headache didn't subside, so I was advised to go home and rest. I was thankful they released me to go home because I'd never experienced a headache like that and wanted to rest. Every time I drove to and from work, I took the same route, but this particular day I decided to go a different route because of traffic on my usual route. About halfway home, I didn't feel well at all. Taking that pill on an empty stomach made me nauseous; I didn't think I could make it home. I decided to get off the highway and go to the closest convenience store to grab a snack to sustain me, hoping it would help my stomach to settle. I grabbed a bag of chips and a drink. I wanted to make it home without being ill and before the freeway got too congested.

As I walked back to my car, that same woman I'd seen the day prior in that parking garage was there. I was now forty miles from that parking garage. I'd already been home and at work since then. This was midday for me; there was absolutely no way that this woman could have followed me. I would have noticed if she followed me—I have a heightened awareness due to a prior accident, which left me always paying close attention to my surroundings when driving. I always check my rearview mirrors when I drive.

The first thing that came out of her mouth (in a creepy voice) was, "Now are you gonna listen to me?" Now I don't know about you, but I was spooked to my core. Like, how in the world did this woman get here? It was the next day in a completely different town, and here I was, encountering the same woman. I was terrified and thought, *"How could this be?"* I got chills up my spine and immediately felt a demonic presence. This woman was not good and came from an evil place, trying to lure me back into the occult, and so I told her that what she was doing was an abomination to the Lord. I explained as quickly as possible that I had just read in the Bible, that what she was offering was not sitting well in my spirit, and that I would not be listening to anything she had to share. I went on to say that maybe if I saw her for a third time, I might listen to her, but I knew in the back of my mind that I wasn't going to. I just wanted to get out of there as quickly as possible.

That was one of the creepiest experiences I've ever had. After that, I knew that the devil, Satan himself, existed and that he had sent one of his earthly demonic messengers to try and draw me back in. He can disguise himself as an angel of light. Satan is real and active and living in this world. He was cast out of Heaven as a fallen angel and is now ruling on Earth in the unseen realm of the spiritual world. I know what you may be thinking, and it's okay to challenge what I'm sharing. But if you were me and were in my shoes, experiencing what I did, you might be able to understand what I'm saying. I also realize that what I'm sharing can be very controversial.

I wanted to share this story with you because as much as I want to share that God is real, I also want to share how the dark side and Satan are also real. Since I am writing

After that, I knew that the devil, Satan himself, existed and that he had sent one of his earthly demonic messengers to try and draw me back in. He can disguise himself as an angel of light.

a book on faith, I think it's important to also speak about how I discovered how real Satan is. Often, and most of the time, the devil is sly in his ways and does not make himself completely known. He comes as an angel of light. The devil is sly and can transform himself into the image of another human being and even a familiar spirit. With that, this lady looked like a typical middle-aged sweet lady based on her outer appearance, which is why it's so important not to assess another individual's motives based on their appearance. This woman was not a threat based on her appearance, but she was someone to be kept away from once she revealed her intent.

I immediately called my close Christian friend when I got home that evening. She'd been heavily involved in the occult and practiced tarot cards before her salvation and relationship with God. I called her to pray for me because I felt such a strong evil presence and was very uncomfortable with what had occurred. She immediately came over with another friend and prayed over me. As they prayed over me, I felt as if something terrible left me. I felt a sense of relief. Thankfully, I have never encountered that woman again, and that was 20 years ago.

This message is about being careful and being on guard against the schemes of Satan because he may come like a light trying to deceive. We are to always be on guard from his wicked schemes. I believe that woman was sent as a demonic messenger to try and deceive me. I am thankful I had been spiritually prepared, having just read that Scripture the night before.

SOMETHING TO CONSIDER

What I just shared was one of the moments that made me aware that there truly is an enemy out to deceive and confuse, and he is completely sly about his tactics. You may even think this is insane or even believe that if it was truly a messenger from Satan, wouldn't it be more of an obvious horror scene with how I was approached? I understand why you might question why I was so certain this was from the dark side. I mean, this lady appeared to come with help and a message that she wanted to share, and how could that be evil, right? I get that thinking, but I want to have you consider that Satan is sly and can appear as an angel of light. He can disguise himself. He is deceptive and tries to lure you in subtle and not-so-obvious ways. He has a way of appearing to be good-natured and cunning, but he is the father of lies and deception.

It is tempting to open spiritual doors that seem harmless to try and figure out answers to life for fun or in times of desperation through tarot cards and mediums. However, God states specifically how we should not entertain these things, and because of that, I knew it was not from God. I understand that in desperate times you may be interested in wanting answers, connecting with deceased loved ones, and needing guidance, and meeting with a psychic medium may seem tempting. I get it because that was also me before becoming a Christian. However, once I knew that doing those things was an abomination to the Lord, I was done seeking anything like that.

If you are still in doubt about what I've shared, go before God and pray about what I've said and ask Him for yourself. Ask Him if going to a fortune teller, medium, or entertaining tarot cards is something that He is okay with. I'm not called to judge anyone who has entertained these things, as I did in my past. Once I knew how God felt about them, I no longer wanted to entertain any of these things. The Scripture I read that week before being approached was given to me as a directive from God, and I had a choice as to whether or not I wanted to engage and listen to that woman, as it was tempting. I knew it was not good and that it was not something God would be pleased with.

DO NOT TURN TO
MEDIUMS OR SEEK OUT
SPIRITISTS, FOR YOU WILL
BE DEFILED BY THEM. I AM
THE LORD YOUR GOD.

—Leviticus 19:31

I WILL BE AGAINST
ANYONE WHO GOES TO
MEDIUMS AND FORTUNE-
TELLERS FOR ADVICE,
BECAUSE THAT PERSON IS
BEING UNFAITHFUL TO ME.
SO, I WILL CUT HIM OFF
FROM HIS PEOPLE.

—Leviticus 20:6 NCV

AND HE MADE HIS SON
PASS THROUGH THE
FIRE, INTERPRETED SIGNS,
PRACTICED DIVINATION,
AND USED MEDIUMS
AND SPIRITISTS. HE
DID GREAT EVIL IN THE
SIGHT OF THE LORD,
PROVOKING HIM TO
ANGER.

—2 Kings 21:6 NASB

AND NO WONDER, FOR
EVEN SATAN DISGUISES
HIMSELF AS AN ANGEL
OF LIGHT. SO, IT IS
NO SURPRISE IF HIS
SERVANTS, ALSO, DISGUISE
THEMSELVES AS SERVANTS
OF RIGHTEOUSNESS. THEIR
END WILL CORRESPOND
TO THEIR DEEDS.

—2 Corinthians 11:14–15 ESV

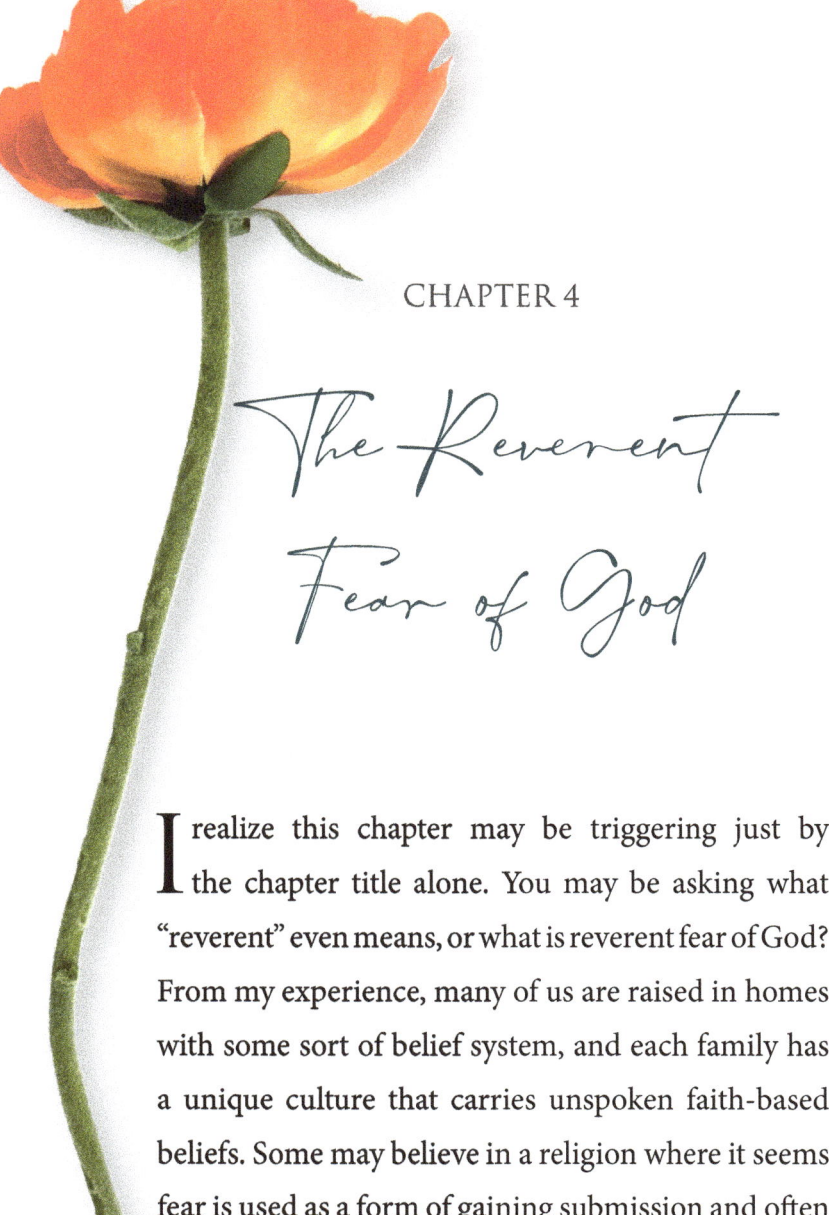

CHAPTER 4

The Reverent Fear of God

I realize this chapter may be triggering just by the chapter title alone. You may be asking what "reverent" even means, or what is reverent fear of God? From my experience, many of us are raised in homes with some sort of belief system, and each family has a unique culture that carries unspoken faith-based beliefs. Some may believe in a religion where it seems fear is used as a form of gaining submission and often isn't demonstrated or spoken in a loving way. You may have been raised with parents or others who have tried to use the "fear of God" to manipulate you to do something they believe you should do. This makes some people fear God or believe He is an unloving authoritative dictator God. You may feel uneasy, wanting to resist God instead of fearing Him.

I get it if you think, "*If God is love, then why would I need to be fearful of Him?*" Great question! When I say "reverent fear," I am talking about a holy kind of fear. A fear that God is the Creator of the world and all things, and so because of that, there is a sense of awe and deep inner belief that God can do anything. However, you may not have been taught about a loving and forgiving God. A God that is to be reverenced as a natural response to knowing how real and loving He truly is. God is mysteriously powerful, and once a person understands what reverent fear of God is, there is an overpowering sense of awe because of His mighty power. Once you have a special encounter with God, you bow down in humility to Him because you *feel* His presence.

When reading the Old Testament, it's easy to interpret that God is a dictator and demanding God, who

This makes some people fear God or believe He is an unloving authoritative dictator God.

is aggressively making direct commands. God can come across to us sometimes as a God who is not loving but harsh instead. God is a God who wanted people to follow His lead and commandments in the Old Testament. However, in the New Testament, He showered His grace and love on us because He planned to come with His love sacrificially. He could have continued in His way, but instead, He showed up in a man, Jesus, to live and die in a sacrificial, loving way.

Although God has never changed, His ways of loving us have become more gracious and merciful. However, based on the title of this chapter, I can understand why you might feel repulsed, irritated, or even anger rising inside of you at the thought of me talking about reverent fear. That is to be expected; I am not surprised by this response. I'm sure God is not surprised by how you think and feel. I believe He welcomes it. He doesn't demand that we believe in Him, which is the beauty of being given free will to accept. He wants us all to believe in Him and have eternal life, but it's not forced. He desires a relationship with us, but entering takes our participation. He wants us to acknowledge His almighty power and ability to do whatever He desires. However, He is a gentle and loving

God, and I believe He wants me to share with you how I developed my reverent fear of Him to shed some new light on and perspective into God's heart.

About five months after I entered into a relationship with God, I was pondering how God could be God, where He came from, and how He could be here from the beginning of time. I worked part-time with my mother, and we drove to our workplace in Laguna Beach, California.

I wanted to share with my mother all the great things I'd experienced since becoming a Christian. I also hoped she'd explore God and possibly enter a relationship with Him. I wanted her to ponder God and His omniscience.

We were driving to work through the canyon, which was beautiful. It was a gorgeous day, and the sky was filled with puffy white clouds, my favorite type of sky. I asked my mother, "Isn't it interesting how God has always existed? I mean, how could God be God and always be here and exist and create all of this? Isn't that amazing?" She agreed, but the conversation was quickly interrupted by a phone call she received. We stopped talking, and I went on to think about something else.

When we arrived at work that day, we did our business as usual until we had a break. I entered my mother's office. She was talking to our co-worker. He stood beside me and spoke to her, using his hands as usual. He was a comedic guy who communicated with his hands and big expressions.

This particular day, I was to his left side as he spoke to my mother about his diabetes. As he talked, he accidentally hit my face and immediately said, "I am so sorry. I'm diabetic. I'm blind in my left eye."

"Of course," I told him, "It's okay," and we went about our day as usual.

Later that day, we drove home about forty miles from our workplace. I frequented the gym most nights to get my workout in. So, after we arrived home, I left to go work out. After doing my usual cardio workout, I needed to use the restroom. Two ladies walked in front of me as I headed into the women's restroom. They appeared to be janitorial staff because they were carrying cleaning supplies. The woman to the right accidentally hit the woman to her left, the same way I was hit earlier that morning. Then she said his exact words: "I am so sorry. I'm diabetic. I'm blind in my left eye." It was as if I was

I asked my mother, "Isn't it interesting how God has always existed? I mean, how could God be God and always be here and exist and create all of this? Isn't that amazing?"

watching a movie in front of me with a repeat of exactly what happened to me five hours earlier.

I immediately heard, *"Now do you see that I can make anything happen? That I can put words in anybody's mouth and have them speak whatever I want?"* I was completely floored. All I wanted to do was lie prostrate on the women's restroom floor. It was as if this anointing reminded me of God's power and power and that He could make anything happen whenever He wanted. God is real, and although we may not see Him, I believe if we seek Him, He will make His presence real. As our Creator, He knows us each individually. He may not reveal Himself in the same way He has to me, but I believe if you want to know if He is real, He will make Himself known to you in a way that only He knows you will be able to receive.

SOMETHING TO CONSIDER

How about you? When you think about God, do you think of Him being powerful and able to do anything He desires to get your attention, as He did for me? I believe God wants to show up in a big and real way in your life. The more you draw close to Him and desire to experience Him in a real and tangible way, He will make Himself

I immediately heard, "Now do you see that I can make anything happen? That I can put words in anybody's mouth and have them speak whatever I want?"

known to you. God wants you to know He is bigger than any struggle, fear, or desperate place you may be in. He wants you to know that He can make anything change that He believes will be for your good.

God probably won't show you His power the same way He did for me, but that is the beauty of God. He is such an intimate God. He is your Creator and knows how to speak to you and get your attention in a way you will receive. I pray that you can sit before Him and ask Him to show you how much He loves you and how real and powerful He is. That can feel scary to some, but I can tell you that it is amazing and exciting. It's better than any high a substance could ever give you. You will be forever changed when you have a personal encounter with God.

Then the Lord opened the donkey's mouth, and it said to Balaam, "What have I done to you to make you beat me these three times?"

Balaam answered the donkey, "You have made a fool of me! If only I had a sword in my hand, I would kill you right now."

The donkey said to Balaam, "Am I not your own donkey, which you have always ridden, to this day? Have I been in the habit of doing this to you?"

"No," he said.

—Numbers 22:28–30

THE FEAR OF THE LORD
IS THE BEGINNING
OF WISDOM, AND
KNOWLEDGE OF THE HOLY
ONE IS UNDERSTANDING.

—Proverbs 9:10

THE FEAR OF THE LORD
IS THE BEGINNING
OF WISDOM; ALL
WHO FOLLOW HIS
PRECEPTS HAVE GOOD
UNDERSTANDING. TO HIM
BELONGS ETERNAL PRAISE.

—Proverbs 111:10

THE FEAR OF THE LORD
LEADS TO LIFE; THEN
ONE RESTS CONTENT,
UNTOUCHED BY TROUBLE.

—Proverbs 19:23

CHAPTER 5

The Marriage Prayer

I t wasn't until I entered a relationship with God that I finally desired more of a godly partnership with the opposite sex. I was often drawn to men and dated out of a desire to be loved. So, until age twenty-five, I sought validation and attention, and my interactions were mainly driven out of pure lust. The relationships were usually short-lived, and it seemed like the men I dated were after one thing, and that was no longer what I was seeking. I was soon tired of painful breakups and the poor decisions I made in my selection process. I gave myself away so easily.

I eventually got to a point where I was emotionally exhausted from dating and only wanted to date to find my forever partner. I needed to face the painful reality that my son's father and I would not get back together. I was heartbroken and not really over him, but I knew I needed to move on. So, when I entered a relationship with God, I prayed that God would heal my heart and remove my desire to be with him. I honestly felt that I would never get married unless I married my son's father. It wasn't until one of my dearest friends got married in the summer of 2003 that I began desiring also to be married. Marriage seemed like such a beautiful union of oneness and divine connectivity.

In the fall of 2003, I started praying for God to bring the right person into my life. I had remained abstinent since I asked God into my heart on June 13, 2002, and I felt finally ready to have God open my heart for the man He had chosen for me. I wanted to be sure that when God chose my forever partner, he would be safe and loving to my son. I knew that my previous selection of men wasn't

I felt finally ready to have God open my heart for the man He had chosen for me. I wanted to be sure that when God chose my forever partner, he would be safe and loving to my son.

led by prayer, and I only wanted to be with someone if God hand-picked him for me and me for him. I was always drawn to different men. Men from other countries usually caught my attention because they were different, not only in their appearance but also in their cultural uniqueness.

One day in November 2003, I ate lunch with some coworkers. I recall telling them that though I had never dated an Asian guy, maybe I was supposed to marry one. I wanted a clear sign of God's approval, so I started earnestly praying for a sign from God. I remember people telling me not to say my prayers out loud because the devil hears what we say if we speak it out, but rather to keep it to myself and pray silently. In addition to praying, I wrote in my journal all the traits and characteristics I desired in a husband.

My prayer to God was extremely specific. I prayed that the man who bought me a cross necklace would be the one God brought me to marry. A week later, I happened to be at the gym, like I would be any other day. I was in the free-weight area I always shied from entering because it was full of young men, and it felt like a meat market full of men hitting on women. It felt like everyone was mostly checking everyone out, from the neck down.

Just as I made my way to place my weight bar back on the rack, this Asian guy smiled and said hello. He looked to be Hawaiian or Filipino. He wasn't my usual type. He looked too full of himself and could probably get any girl he wanted. He had a smaller waist than me and was bulging with muscles from head to toe—one of those typical guys you would see practically living in the gym.

Next thing you know, he approached me, asking me out for coffee. What's funny is that I told my friends that if a guy asked me out to a bar for a drink, I would say no. However, I'd say yes if he asked me out for coffee. Well, I gave in and took him up on his invitation, but not without quite the earful to try and turn him off. I told him I was boring and lived a boring life—that I just worked and came to the gym, was a Christian, and only dated Christians. I even went to the extreme and gave him the full disclosure upfront—I wouldn't have sex before marriage. His response was hilarious. He said, "Geeze, I just wanted coffee. And I'm Catholic. Does that count as being Christian?"

Well, needless to say, I gave in. We started dating and realized we had a lot in common. Believe it or not, he matched all the desired traits and characteristics of a forever partner I had written down in my journal. I mean *all* of them. It seemed we were a match made in Heaven and were inseparable. We spent any free time we had together.

One night after our usual gym workout, he came over. He seemed a bit nervous and said he had something to give me. He said he had an early Christmas gift and was too excited to keep it—he wanted me to have it early. I opened the box to find a white gold cross necklace. I was in shock. He probably wondered what I was thinking. If he'd known, he might have run right back out the door with the gift in hand. I was freaking out, thinking, *Oh my gosh, God, this is him?! My future husband.*

He saw how excited I looked and said, "I went with the intention to buy you a heart pendant, but something told me to buy you this cross necklace. It was the only cross necklace in the case. I hope you like it."

He hoped I liked it.

He had no idea how I felt and what thoughts raced through my head. At the time, we had only been dating for a month. Then I told him the prayer I had prayed. He proposed two months later and within seven months, we were married.

I believe it's important to share that we went through premarital counseling for about six months, which was required in our church if we wanted our church to marry us. They wanted to ensure we were truly prepared for marriage, as they felt responsible to God for vouching for our marriage. In the first session, I told the pastor my prayer, and he suggested I pray and get confirmation of my prayer in the Bible from God's word.

The very next day, I intentionally arrived at work a little early to be able to pray and read my Bible, as I desperately wanted to hear confirmation from God if this man was truly to be my husband. I parked my car and prayed, asking God to show me a Scripture in the Bible to confirm if he was to be my husband. I opened up to a random page and just started reading. It was in the book of Genesis, chapter 24, verses 12 to 20. It was a marriage prayer asking God for a sign. The woman who comes and offers water not only to Abraham's servant but to his camels as well is the woman to marry Isaac. This was my confirmation from the Bible. The beautiful thing was that the confirmation came to me a day later, and I opened right to it without digging through the Bible.

SOMETHING TO CONSIDER

Whether you look at marriage as a forever binding covenant like the Bible states or as a contractual agreement, marriage is marriage. When you say, "I do," and enter into a marital union with your partner, it's a serious decision and not one that we want to make hastily. While I know I made mine quickly, it was first brought to God. I wanted to make sure that the person I decided to marry was divinely selected, stamped with God's approval. I believe that He is the knower of all, the Creator of the universe and each of us, and I wanted to make sure that the person I chose to say "I do" to was God's will for me. I urge you to do the same.

If you desire to be married or are even dating, I highly suggest you go to God in prayer and seek answers from Him regarding the people you not only spend time with but especially enter into a marital union with. This is a person with whom you will share in life's most challenging and intimate moments. You will journey through wonderful, harmonious, stormy, discouraging times with them. You want to be able to say, "We're a match made in Heaven."

These were the verses I opened up to when I asked God to confirm my husband. I read:

> "Then he prayed, 'Lord, God of my master Abraham, make me successful today, and show kindness to my master Abraham. See, I am standing beside this spring, and the daughters of the townspeople are coming out to draw water. May it be that when I say to a young woman, "Please let down your jar that I may have a drink," and she says, "Drink, and I'll water your camels too"—let her be the one you have chosen for your servant Isaac. By this, I will know that you have shown kindness to my master.' Before he had finished praying, Rebekah came out with her jar on her shoulder. She was the daughter of Bethuel son of Milkah, who was the wife of Abraham's brother Nahor. The woman was very beautiful, a virgin; no man had ever slept with her. She went down to the spring, filled her jar, and came up again. The servant hurried to meet her and said, 'Please give me a little water from your jar.' 'Drink, my lord,' she said, and quickly lowered the jar to her hands and gave him a

*drink. After she had given him a drink, she said,
'I'll draw water for your camels too, until they
have had enough to drink.' So, she quickly
emptied her jar into the trough, ran back
to the well to draw more water, and drew enough
for all his camels."*

–Genesis 24:12–20 NLT

CHAPTER 6

The Dream That Saved My Youngest Son

Three years after being married to my husband, we were blessed with the gift of conceiving a child. We both wanted a child together and felt ready, so we began praying that if it were God's will for us to have a baby, we would. But if not, to take the desire away from us. Being pregnant was a joy, and I truly enjoyed every moment. I can't complain about either of my pregnancies, other than at the end of them, I became tired and gained too much weight. I feel for those who've gone through challenging pregnancies or haven't yet been able to conceive. I can only imagine how difficult that is, and I don't take my experience for granted.

During my last trimester, as part of the protocol, my doctor highly encouraged me to take CPR and Lamaze classes before giving birth. The day before the class, I was exhausted and considered not going. I'd already had one child and knew how to do this. But the night before the class, I had a terrifying dream. I dreamt that my son was in his crib choking, and I didn't know how to resuscitate him—and he ended up dying. I woke up from my dream mortified. It felt so real. It scared me so much that I decided to attend the CPR class, and I am so thankful I did.

Due to all the talk about SIDS (Sudden Infant Death Syndrome), I never had peace placing our son in his crib away from us for his first year. Now, everybody has the right to raise their children how they see fit and that they're comfortable with, and I would never judge anybody for how they feel they need to be with their

I dreamt that my son was in his crib choking, and I didn't know how to resuscitate him—and he ended up dying. I woke up from my dream mortified. It scared me so much that I decided to attend the CPR class, and I am so thankful I did.

children. I chose to co-sleep or at least have my baby next to our bed in his bassinet.

When our son was five months old, we dedicated him to God in our church. Our son seemed to have a slight cold and cough. We had taken him to his pediatrician and he was prescribed Benadryl for his nasal congestion and Rondec-DM for his cough. We gave it to him the day following his baby dedication. The pharmacist said that we could give him the meds, then my husband rushed out the door to make it to work on time.

Since we had just given him the medications, I wanted to feed him to get something in his stomach. I was lying sideways, facing him on my side and feeding him with the bottle. I was exhausted and began to doze off. I was immediately woken up twenty minutes later as I felt his body tense up and stiffen. He was having a seizure, and I was utterly terrified. It's interesting how you must be present and strong in emergencies, no matter how afraid you are. I remembered hearing that if someone is seizing, to leave them—make sure they are on their side, but not to move them. So, I tried my best to leave him there to have his seizure while watching every moment in despair, praying it would end.

After what seemed like ten minutes, but which was probably only thirty seconds, his face turned a bluish-gray color. I quickly picked him up and began the Heimlich maneuver I learned in the CPR class. I prayed desperately, pleading with God to please not take my baby. I tried to stay focused through my emotions, continuing to perform the Heimlich over both legs and going back and forth.

I finally heard him take a gasp of air and start breathing. I immediately got up and called 911. Thankfully, our son was okay and is still okay today. However, that was one of my life's most devastating and terrifying days. All of that to say, I believe God gave me that dream months prior as a gift to prepare me for that very day. Had I not attended that CPR class, I wouldn't have known what to do that day.

If I had put our son to bed in his crib, he would have passed away, and doctors would have likely said it was SIDS. All I can say is that I am so thankful that he was next to me that day.

I believe that God speaks to us through visions and dreams, and they are often the revelation and mystery of things to come in our lives. Sometimes He will bring

I believe God gave me that dream months prior as a gift to prepare me for that very day. Had I not attended that CPR class, I wouldn't have known what to do that day.

dreams that have spiritual meaning for us. In my case, it was a warning dream for me to take that CPR class because if I hadn't gone that day, I would have lost my child.

SOMETHING TO CONSIDER

You may have dreams. Some might be prophetic to tell you about things in the future. You won't know until the dream comes to pass. It may freak you out, or it can bring you peace. Either way, you may have vivid dreams as I did, and I want you to pay attention to those dreams. Don't be too quick to dismiss dreams as if they are meaningless.

Now, some dreams may not be significant. Not every dream is meant to guide you; it could be your mind's way of releasing the thoughts you've had throughout the day. However, if you get vivid dreams that usually come to fruition or tend to guide you somehow, I urge you not to disregard them. I encourage you to pray to God after a dream, not just go to a friend or a dream interpretation book. Although that can be intriguing, you must be careful when reading other people's dream interpretations. Instead, go to God directly and ask Him to interpret your dream. I believe He will let you know whether your dream is something of significance or not. As we read in the Bible, God gave dreams to many people as warnings, prophesies, or to speak a message into that person's life. God is the same yesterday, today, and tomorrow, and He often does give people messages through dreams and visions. Please do not ignore your dreams but pray to God about them.

THEN THE MYSTERY WAS
REVEALED TO DANIEL IN
A NIGHT VISION. THEN
DANIEL BLESSED THE
GOD OF HEAVEN.

—Daniel 2:19 ESV

CHAPTER 7

The Calling

We all go into marriage with expectations of how we think it should look. My marriage needed a sort of revival for me to stay married. At the time, I had been married for a little over seven years. I was having a difficult time because I felt I couldn't continue my marriage the way it was going. My husband and I had a lot of emotional maturing to do, and we often reacted out of our emotions and had difficulty regulating them. We were constantly repeating toxic communication cycles and would get flooded. Our disagreements often escalated and turned into my husband raising his voice, becoming verbally abusive, and dismissing my feelings. I began to feel like I didn't have a voice in my marriage, pressing me toward wanting a separation. All of my well-meaning Christian friends, along with my therapist at that time, continued to tell me that I did not need to stay in a verbally abusive marriage; however, I wanted to make sure that I was hearing from God directly before I made any drastic decisions to leave my marriage.

In January 2012, I decided to put my real estate career aside and focus on returning to college to pursue my education. My husband encouraged me to go back and get my associate degree at the time. I scheduled a meeting with a school counselor and started the only interesting class left. It was a lifespan psychology course. The first two months of the class discussed the stages of life from birth through adolescence, and that is when I realized that I have a heart for children. I realized I wanted to advocate for children. That was where the first seed was planted, but I had no idea how that would manifest in my life.

A few months had passed. It was April 14, 2012. It was a Saturday night, and I decided to attend a church service alone because my husband and I had been arguing. I

My husband and I had a lot of emotional maturing to do, and we often reacted out of our emotions and had difficulty regulating them. We were constantly repeating toxic communication cycles and would get flooded.

wanted to hear something directly from God and needed direction on what to do in my marriage, whether to stay or go. Meanwhile, I had secretly stashed separation paperwork in the trunk of my car without my husband knowing that I wanted to separate from him and that I had been praying and crying out to God for months.

This particular night I was really engaged in the message. I recall the pastor sharing his testimony of flipping houses, and as clear as day, I heard, "You're going to have an orphanage one day in the middle of a forest." I knew it was God speaking to me. It was a distinctive, soft, stern, yet loving tone. It felt like I had been walking in a dry, hot desert for years, parched, when I suddenly got a drink of the coldest, most refreshing glass of water.

Although I doubted myself, I felt a sense of divine purpose, a calling to attention, and divine direction for my life. I immediately responded, "God, look at my life— you know I had a child out of wedlock, and I struggle as a mother. How could I ever have an orphanage?"

Immediately, I heard this response from God: "Lisa, you know I can do anything with your life." I responded with reverence because, as I mentioned in Chapter 4, I knew that when He said something, He meant it. I knew that I could believe Him at His word. He had repeatedly shown me that when He says something, it will happen, and that I needed to stop doubting my abilities because God would make me able if He willed to do so. Also, to confirm I heard it from God, I kept it to myself.

Three days later, my husband woke up from a dream. Mind you, he never shared his dreams with me, and on this particular day, he did. He said, "I had the weirdest dream last night. I never remember my dreams, but this dream was so vivid."

I responded, "Oh yeah, what did you dream about?"

He said, "We had an orphanage; all I remember was greenery everywhere. It was green all around us, and all these dark-skinned boys wanted a mohawk haircut."

"Really?" I asked. "Did you see my older son or our younger son?" He said that my older son was not in his dream but that he saw our younger son, who appeared to be about sixteen or seventeen. He went on to share that our younger son was telling all the boys to line up to get their haircuts by my husband, who, for the record, does not cut hair as his profession. That was when I completely froze and thought to myself, *WOW! This is confirmation, God.* Then I felt God wanted me to share what He had

Clear as day, I heard. "You're going to have an orphanage one day in the middle of a forest." I knew it was God speaking to me. It was a distinctive, soft, stern, yet loving tone.

told me in church three nights prior. My husband was super surprised and could hardly believe it.

The word given to me and confirmed to my husband in his dream kept me focused on school. Not only did it speak to me about God wanting me to stay in my marriage, but God's future calling to have an orphanage was not only spoken to me but was confirmed to my husband. The fact that God gave me the word and then confirmed it to my husband was an answered prayer that God desired me to stay in my marriage. Additionally, I knew that there was a purpose for my school journey and that I needed to continue my education. Overall, the word God spoke to me that evening in church has kept me in my marriage, even when rough times have come because no marriage is perfect. It has also given me a purpose and direction, which I refer to as a "calling" for my life.

SOMETHING TO CONSIDER

Marriage is a sacred and powerful union. It is the most intimate example of God's relationship with us. If you are in a difficult marriage and feel you want out, pray to God. He is the Mighty and Best Counselor to guide you, but also get wise, godly counsel. And pray, pray,

Three days later, my husband woke up from a dream. He said, "I had the weirdest dream last night. I never remember my dreams, but this dream was so vivid . . . We had an orphanage; all I remember was greenery everywhere."

pray. Before deciding about moving toward separation or divorce, pray and wait on God, as He will guide you in the direction you should take. Don't be in a hurry to go straight to separation or divorce, as you may have a lot to consider. You may have children or strong emotional or financial ties. Make sure that at the end of it all, no matter your decision, you have peace from God that He was the one who agreed to your decision. One day, we will all give account for our choices. You want to make sure that every decision is brought to God in prayer, especially leaving a marriage.

This is the Scripture reference that kept me in prayer about what I was going through in my marriage:

> *"'Haven't you read,' he replied, 'that at the beginning the Creator "made them male and female," and said, "For this reason, a man will leave his father and mother and be united to his wife, and the two will become one flesh?" So, they are no longer two, but one flesh. Therefore, what God has joined together, let no one separate.'*
>
> *'Why then,' they asked, 'did Moses command that a man give his wife a certificate of divorce and send her away?'*

Jesus replied, 'Moses permitted you to divorce your wives because your hearts were hard. But it was not this way from the beginning. I tell you that anyone who divorces his wife, except for sexual immorality, and marries another woman commits adultery."

—Matthew 19:4–9

**I'm not passing judgment on anyone considering leaving or who has already left, as that is not my place, and I would never judge you. God is the only judge.

Closing Message

Whether you are questioning God's existence, praying to have faith or hope, or needing encouragement, I hope that at least one of these short stories somehow touched your life. These seven short stories are real and profound. They have been the monumental moments that have ignited my faith in God. They are something I felt I should share and not keep to myself, as I believe all we go through is not just for us but to comfort others.

You may feel alienated, lost, confused, and without hope or peace. You may feel as though life has nothing of substance to offer, a void within you that nothing else seems to satisfy. You may be wondering if you should stay or leave a relationship. For any of those situations, I hope and pray you are inspired to seek God with all your heart, as He is waiting for you to enter into a relationship with Him through His only begotten Son, Jesus Christ. The journey of walking with God has been the best decision. I'm unsure where I would have ended up without Him giving me the gift of receiving His divine love and acceptance, which has transformed my life from the inside out. The gift of receiving the Holy Spirit to guide and lead me into all truth has anchored me and filled the void in my life that was once there. I no longer feel lost or without peace. Aside from these stories, there are many more, but these were the big ones that I felt God wanted me to share with all of you.

> *Praise be to the God and Father of our Lord Jesus Christ, the Father of compassion and the God of all comfort, who comforts us in all our troubles, so that we can comfort those in any trouble with the comfort we ourselves receive from God.*
>
> —2 Corinthians 1:3–4

CLOSING MESSAGE

*If you declare with your mouth, "Jesus is
Lord," and believe in your heart that God raised
Him from the dead, you will be saved.*

—Romans 10:9

*Jesus answered, "I am the way and the truth and
the life. No one comes to the Father except
through me."*

—John 14:6

*Peace I leave with you; My peace I give you. I do
not give to you as the world gives. Do not let your
hearts be troubled and do not be afraid.*

—John 14:27

Now I want to share the practical steps I took to help start you on this journey, the best decision you'll ever make. I'm not promising that it will always be easy, but you must decide if you want to live for yourself or God—to please people or God. Suppose you want to die or live eternally when you pass away. I can promise you this: the peace and joy you will feel is better than any substance or replacement you may have tried to cope with.

So, here are the steps I suggest you take:

1. Pray the Sinner's Prayer, the prayer mentioned in John 3. The prayer below is for you to pray if you have decided you are ready to enter into a relationship with your Creator. I also recommend praying for God to remove everything from your life that is not His best for you, whether it be people or passions that you have.

2. You'll want to get a study Bible. I started with the new American Standard Bible in the study version; however, if you go to the local bookstore, like Barnes & Noble or a local bookstore, you can look through all the study Bibles and see which one you prefer.

3. Pray and ask the Holy Spirit where He wants you to start reading the Bible. I was advised to start in the book of John. Then, I read through the book of Hebrews, which is all about having faith. Then you can read one psalm and one proverb every day. I read a proverb every day of the month. Please keep in mind that it's not a race. You want to take your time. Always pray before you read. You might even want to highlight or keep a journal and a pen near you for anything that stands out for your faith walk.

4. Try to attend a local Christian church.

5. You may want to look into getting water baptized, but again, let the Holy Spirit guide you because if you were baptized when you were a baby or little, you didn't have a choice. Now that you've decided, you may re-dedicate yourself to God and get baptized again. Let the Holy Spirit lead you in that.

6. You may also want to get prayed over and ask to be baptized in the Holy Spirit. Remember that not all churches believe this needs to be done, so pray and ask God if He thinks you should have this prayer over you by elders or those gifted in prayer, with a prayer ministry to pray over you.

7. Get plugged in. Join a Bible study and surround yourself with other people in the faith. God tells us not to forsake assembling with others as it builds each other up.

Remember that this is a journey. Some people will experience radical transformation immediately, while others experience it in smaller doses. Remember that God knows what's best for you, and each of us is unique. Not one person has the same fingerprint; that is how intricate our God is.

If you want to enter into a relationship with your Creator, I would like to share with you the prayer I prayed, that you can also pray to make the best life decision. God is not a forceful God, and He gives us all a choice to believe in Him or not, but if you want to enter into that relationship, here is the prayer:

Dear Jesus,
Please forgive all my sins that I have committed,
both knowingly and unknowingly. I believe You
came to this earth as God in the flesh and died on
the cross for my sins and eternal life. I give You my
life and ask that You come into my heart and give
me the gift of the Holy Spirit to guide me and lead
me to all truth. I surrender my life to You and ask
You to take everything out of my life that is not
good or Your will for me. Please give me spiritual
understanding so I may continue to walk with
You and understand what Your spirit is trying to
say to me when reading the Bible. In Jesus' name,
amen.

About the Author

L isa Soriano has been walking with God as a Christian for over 20 years, surrendering her life to Jesus Christ and entering that relationship on June 13, 2002. She got married shortly after in August 2004. Lisa has two children and a daughter-in-law. She continues to live a life led by and anchored in her faith. Although her journey has not been easy, she has chosen to stay in the race of life, relying on God for everything, staying on her number, and not giving up.

Lisa is devoted to God, first and foremost, as well as her family and loved ones. She has a strong passion and desire to help others heal. Lisa is a Licensed Clinical Social Worker (LCSW), practicing in

California as a psychotherapist, and has been in the field for over six years.

After becoming licensed, Lisa opened her private practice, Anchored & Armored Therapeutic Services. Lisa's passion and driving force have developed from living a life led by the Holy Spirit. Therefore, she wants to share God's love and faithfulness to the world, to inspire many, while imparting faith and hope to all.

Lisa has lived life with many blessings and challenges that have helped shape her life, inspiring her to want to share her stories with all of you in hopes that something might help you along your journey in life. She hopes to either plant a seed of faith in you or water a seed of faith that has already been planted.

God is an intimate God who knows us individually and operates in mysterious ways. Lisa is excited to share her personal experiences, hoping they help you along your journey in life. As a person of faith who struggled many years without having faith in God, or anything for that matter, she would like to share some of the most powerful moments that ignited and maintained her faith.

If this book has touched you in any way, please email Lisa at lisasorianolcsw@gmail.com.

IF YOU ENJOYED THIS BOOK, WILL YOU HELP ME SPREAD THE WORD?

There are several ways you can help me get the word out about the message of this book:

1. Post a 5-Star review on Amazon.
2. Share the book on your Blog, Facebook, Twitter, Instagram, LinkedIn—any social media you regularly use!
3. Recommend the book to friends—word-of-mouth is still the most effective form of advertising.
4. Purchase additional copies to give away as gifts.

The best way to connect is by visiting
https://www.lisasorianolcsw.com

NEED A DYNAMIC SPEAKER FOR YOUR NEXT EVENT?

The best way to connect with me is by emailing lisasorianolcsw@gmail.com or visiting https://www.lisasorianolcsw.com

www.ingramcontent.com/pod-product-compliance
Lightning Source LLC
Chambersburg PA
CBHW051627120626
46551CB00014B/1969